Energy Systems Integration Facility (ESIF) External Stakeholders Workshop: Workshop Proceedings, 9 October 2008, Golden, Colorado

National Renewable Energy Laboratory (NREL)

National Renewable Energy Laboratory

Innovation for Our Energy Future

A national laboratory of the U.S. Department of Energy
Office of Energy Efficiency & Renewable Energy

Energy Systems Integration Facility (ESIF) External Stakeholders Workshop

Workshop Proceedings

Proceedings
NREL/TP-581-44249
January 2009

C. Komomua, B. Kroposki, D. Mooney, T. Stoffel,
B. Parsons, S. Hammond, C. Kutscher, R. Remick,
G. Sverdrup, R. Hawsey, and M. Pacheco
National Renewable Energy Laboratory

Golden Colorado
October 9, 2008

NREL is operated for DOE by the Alliance for Sustainable Energy, LLC   Contract No. DE-AC36-08-GO28308

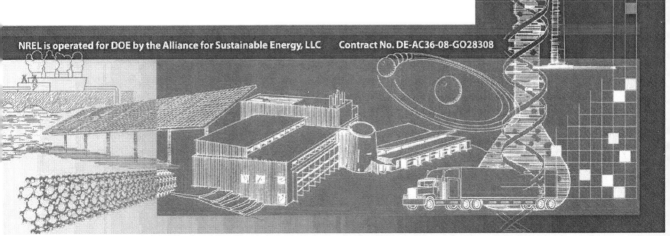

Energy Systems Integration Facility (ESIF) External Stakeholders Workshop

Workshop Proceedings

C. Komomua, B. Kroposki, D. Mooney, T. Stoffel,
B. Parsons, S. Hammond, C. Kutscher, R. Remick,
G. Sverdrup, R. Hawsey, and M. Pacheco
National Renewable Energy Laboratory

Golden Colorado
October 9, 2008

Prepared under Task No. IGIN.7400

Proceedings
NREL/TP-581-44249
January 2009

National Renewable Energy Laboratory
1617 Cole Boulevard, Golden, Colorado 80401-3393
303-275-3000 • www.nrel.gov

NREL is a national laboratory of the U.S. Department of Energy
Office of Energy Efficiency and Renewable Energy
Operated by the Alliance for Sustainable Energy, LLC

Contract No. DE-AC36-08-GO28308

Acknowledgements

Special thanks to our Keynote Speaker, Robert McGrath, and all of the workshop speakers and participants who contributed their time, knowledge, and feedback on the design plans of the Energy Systems Integration Facility.

We would also like to extend our sincere appreciation to Melissa Muffett and David Glickson who were instrumental in organizing and coordinating the workshop activities, and Technical Communicators Jennifer Elling, Howard Brown, Julie Tuttle, and Jennifer Josey, who did an excellent job recording participant discussions during the group breakout sessions.

Executive Summary

Critical to the successful design of the Department of Energy's (DOE) planned Energy Systems Integration Facility (ESIF) is input related to the functional requirements from key external stakeholders such as other national laboratories, industry, and utilities. To establish a formal framework for feedback, on October 9, 2008, stakeholder partners and various national labs across the country gathered to volunteer their time and efforts to provide feedback on the proposed design and functionality of the ESIF. The *Energy Systems Integration Facility External Stakeholders Workshop* was held in Golden, Colorado, and sponsored by the National Renewable Energy Laboratory (NREL).

The full-day workshop was designed to encourage discussion by a variety of different stakeholders on key issues related to the ESIF to ensure that the design of the facility effectively addresses the most critical barriers to large-scale energy efficiency and renewable energy deployment. To that end, the workshop goals were to:

- Raise awareness for key stakeholders regarding future plans and capabilities

- Ensure that the building design and functionality addresses key stakeholder needs

- Solicit feedback on the functionality of the facility for future design consideration

- Lay foundations for collaborations using the ESIF capabilities.

The workshop began with opening remarks from Robert McGrath, NREL's Deputy Director for Research, Development, and Demonstration. He began by thanking all the participants for attending the workshop. He then introduced NREL's new management and operations (M&O) contract recipient and provided a high level overview of the significance of the planned ESIF.

The M&O contract was recently awarded by DOE to Alliance for Sustainable Energy, LLC (Alliance). A newly established limited liability corporation, Alliance is a 50/50 partnership between Battelle Memorial Institute and Midwest Research Institute.

Reducing dependence on imported oil through enhanced efficiencies and bringing renewable energy options to market are key elements of NREL's missions that are vital to the nation's energy and security interests. The new ESIF is a cornerstone facility, supporting NREL's plans for integrating new technologies into the nation's energy infrastructure. The EISF will enable a fully integrated and comprehensive approach to treating the nation's infrastructure as a whole system comprised of many interdependent subsystems ranging from energy generation to transmission to distribution to end use. This approach will identify and more rapidly overcome physical, technological, and operational barriers to large-scale deployment of new technologies so innovations can move from concept to consumers more rapidly at lower costs and with lower risks.

The plenary sessions went next, followed by facilitated breakout sessions, and the workshop concluded with breakout session summaries and a group discussion on collaboration and industry partnership.

The plenary sessions included the following presentations:

- ESIF Overview, David Mooney, Director, Electricity Resources & Building Systems Integration Center

- ESIF Design Requirement Identification, Benjamin Kroposki, Group Manager, Distributed Energy Systems Integration

- Renewable Resource Characterization, Tom Stoffel, Principal Group Manager, Resource Measurements & Forecasting

- Distributed Systems Integration and Operation, Benjamin Kroposki, Group Manager, Distributed Energy Systems Integration

- Transmissions Systems Integration and Operation, Brian Parsons, Program Manager, Transmissions Systems Integration

- Modeling, Simulation, and Data Management, Steven Hammond, Director, Computational Sciences Center

- Buildings and Thermal Systems, Chuck Kutscher, Group Manager, Thermal Systems

- Hydrogen Technologies, Robert Remick, Director, Hydrogen Technologies & Systems Center

During the facilitated breakout sessions, participants were asked to answer four major design questions:

1. What are the top integration priorities that DOE and the ESIF should address to enable high penetration of energy efficiency and renewable energy technology?

2. How can the ESIF's design be best optimized to add value to your efforts in accelerating technology R&D, adoption, and integration?

3. Do we have the right functionality and set of capabilities identified to address the top integration priorities?

4. How can we best ensure sustained stakeholder input throughout the design/build and startup/fit-up process?

Also on the agenda was the issue of effective partnering and finding ways to successfully engage groups of industries and companies in pre-competitive R&D. The Collaboration and Industry Partnerships discussion lead by Michael Pacheco, Vice President, Deployment & Industrial Partnerships, provided direction on laying the groundwork to better facilitate industry partnerships in order to increase and maximize the impact of the ESIF.

While this report provides a summary of the plenary session and details of the breakout sessions, and reports on the answers to the four design questions, this Executive Summary reports on related key topics that emerged throughout the day as reported by Robert Hawsey, Associate Lab Director, Electricity & End Use Systems, in his closing remarks.

Living Laboratory

The ESIF building should be a living laboratory where the performance of the facility's components and systems will be optimized for minimizing energy use in addition to the cutting-edge research being conducted in the building. Next steps will be to consider how to implement the living laboratory ideas within the ESIF and what types of added features to the design of the building, such as onsite storage, advanced meter infrastructure, and submetering, will further support this initiative.

Human Factor Design

From the "human" angle, there was a fair amount of discussion about the interaction of people from utilities, industry, labs, and universities that will be utilizing the research capabilities and the energy efficient strategies of the building. Recommendations included benchmarking from stakeholders that have incorporated a "human factors" design standard into their offices. For example, Southern California Edison's (SCE) Office of the Future is designed to be a sustainable building that saves energy while improving livability for its employees. As the planning stage for the office space in the ESIF continues, stakeholders should take advantage of what the ESIF partnerships have learned thus far.

The workshop participants also discussed incorporating plug-in hybrid electric vehicle (PHEV) charging capability for employees and visitors who may be "early adopters" of plug-in vehicles.

Actionable Information

Participants agreed that the ESIF outputs cannot simply be databases posted on the Internet. The ESIF needs to act as a central "data hub and visualization center" that provides actionable and interactive information that informs and enables technology and integration decisions.

Energy Efficiency and Renewable Energy Technologies

The ESIF design needs to ensure the appropriate balance between renewable and efficiency technology and utilize current partnerships with utilities, system integrators and component developers by taking advantage of their interests and expertise in the energy carriers: electricity (distributed generation, intelligent demand-side controls, and demand response technologies) and hydrogen (generation, storage, and use).

System of Systems Model
The ESIF has a unique capability of enhancing its integration mission with the application of a System of Systems Model incorporating generation, transmission, and distribution technologies for electricity and hydrogen with end-use technologies and the built environment.

Reinvent Data Center Operations
The ESIF has the opportunity to reinvent how data centers are designed, built, and operated. The design of the high-performance computer and data center should establish benchmarks based on other labs (TEAM Initiative) for data center efficiency and rely on the DOE's Industrial Technologies Program (ITP) for decision tools and expertise. Direct current distribution to the computers should be explored, and mechanical cooling should be eliminated. Novel techniques implemented that improve the energy performance of the data center should be broadly disseminated.

Partnerships and Collaborations
A key area of discussion surrounded partnering strategies or models that would be most effective in developing working partnerships at the ESIF. There was significant interest in both developing new models and taking advantage of models that DOE's Hydrogen and Vehicle Technologies Programs, DoD's Defense Advanced Research Projects Agency, and other organizations have already developed, such as the Solid State Energy Convergence Alliance and the USAutoPARTS model. Key model elements must include high-level, sponsor-defined outcomes and a structure that meets the various requirements for all parties. Recommendations also included looking at how trade organizations like the American Society of Heating, Refrigerating, and Air-Conditioning Engineers (ASHRAE), Solar Electric Power Association (SEPA), National Hydrogen Association (NHA), and the American Wind Energy Association (AWEA) sponsor pre-competitive R&D.

Table of Contents

1   Introduction

As the National Renewable Energy Laboratory (NREL) executes its research, development, demonstration, and deployment (RDD&D) missions, input from the national community collectively responsible for developing new energy technologies and for driving them to market is a critical element of its success. On October 9, 2008, NREL hosted a workshop to provide an opportunity for external stakeholders to offer insights and recommendations on the design and functionality of DOE's planned Energy Systems Infrastructure Facility (ESIF). The goal was to ensure that the planning for the ESIF effectively addresses the most critical barriers to large-scale energy efficiency (EE) and renewable energy (RE) deployment. To that end, the purpose of the *Energy Systems Integration Facility External Stakeholders Workshop* was to:

- Raise awareness for key stakeholders regarding future plans and capabilities

- Ensure that the building design and functionality addresses key stakeholder needs

- Solicit feedback on the functionality of the facility for future design modifications

- Lay foundations for collaborations using the ESIF capabilities.

More than 60 people attended the workshop representing industry, the Federal government, and various national labs across the country.

2   Opening Remarks

Robert McGrath, Deputy Director for Research, Development, and Demonstration, began by thanking all the participants attending the workshop. He then introduced NREL's new management and operations (M&O) contract recipient and provided a high level overview of the significance of the planned ESIF.

The M&O contract was recently awarded by DOE to Alliance for Sustainable Energy, LLC. A newly established limited liability corporation, Alliance is a 50/50 partnership between Battelle Memorial Institute and Midwest Research Institute, two partners that have a long history of working together at NREL.

Reducing dependence on imported oil through enhanced efficiencies and bringing renewable energy options to market are key elements of NREL's missions that are vital to the nation's comprehensive strategy. The new ESIF is a cornerstone facility, supporting NREL's plans for integrating new technologies into the nation's energy infrastructure. The EISF will enable a fully integrated and comprehensive approach to treating the nation's infrastructure as a whole system comprised of many interdependent subsystems ranging from energy generation to distribution to end use. This approach will identify and more rapidly overcome physical, technological, and operational barriers to large-scale deployment of new technologies so innovations can move from concept to consumers at lower costs and with lower risks.

The plenary sessions came next, followed by facilitated breakout sessions, and the workshop concluded with breakout session summaries and a group discussion on collaboration and industry partnerships (see Appendix A for the Workshop Agenda).

3   Summary of Plenary Session Presentations

The plenary session consisted of seven speaker presentations and included an overview of the ESIF, Design Requirement Identification, and five specific topic area presentations that set the stage for issues to be addressed during the breakout sessions:

- Renewable Resource Characterization
- Distributed Systems Integration and Operation
- Transmission Systems Integration and Operation
- Modeling, Simulation, and Data Management
- Buildings and Thermal Systems
- Hydrogen Technology.

The PowerPoint presentations for each of the following plenary sessions are available by contacting Melissa Muffett at melissa_muffett@nrel.gov.

3.1   ESIF Overview
Presented by David Mooney, Director, Electricity, Resources and Building Systems Integration Center, the ESIF Overview provided background on the ESIF and its vision going forward.

As the rates of deployment increase, the scale of RE and EE deployment increase, and the costs are reduced, supporting technologies will require a number of unique characteristics that are not found in today's energy infrastructure. Large penetrations of these technologies into the market present a number of challenges in integrating them into existing technologies, and there are a number of issues that need to be considered so these unique operating characteristics do not become barriers to high penetration. As these challenges are identified, the capabilities to address them must be identified. As penetration levels for these technologies increase, the issues should be addressed now instead of 5, 10, or 15 years down the road.

Some foreseeable integration challenges for electricity and hydrogen include:

- Generation variability
- Generation dispatchability
- Distributed special resource, sometimes remote with little or no transmission
- New infrastructure and communications requirements
- Interoperability with existing systems
- Integration with other SmartGrid technologies.

The ESIF stakeholders need to be able to fully assess the system as a whole—a system made up of many interacting and interdependent subsystems—and realize the performance and reliability impacts of the whole system up and down the infrastructure, from integration to end use. Knowing how systems react under different operating and geographic conditions will reduce operating uncertainties and the risk of integrating EE and RE technologies.

A new energy infrastructure paradigm presents two challenges for the ESIF: What happens when these new technologies and parts of the system start to interact in unpredicted ways? And given a new set of natural resources and demand profile, what is the optimized set of technology solutions for each part of that system?

For electricity, the ESIF stakeholders need to consider the real value of different types of load control and energy storage to the overall system. The operations and optimization of these systems should be validated to show the benefits of these solutions for distributed and bulk renewable and efficient energy technologies.

For hydrogen, the ESIF stakeholders need to consider hydrogen production, storage, delivery, and use including the interaction between electric and hydrogen infrastructure.

The design of the functionality and capabilities of the ESIF presents significant and challenging issues, and as the project proceeds, stakeholders will need to maintain a "whole system" concept spanning the entire energy infrastructure.

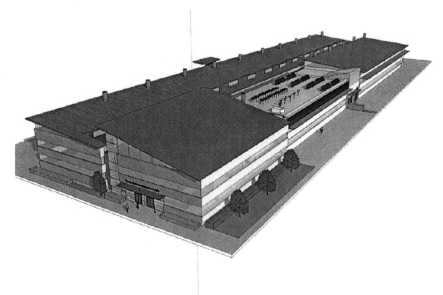

Figure 1-1: Artist's rendering of the ESIF facility.

The vision of the ESIF on the highest level is to enable complex systems research and development that fully integrates the most advanced simulation, data analysis, engineering, and evaluation techniques to transform the nation's energy infrastructure.

The 130,000 sq. ft. facility will be home to various laboratories and offices. Currently, there is no official design of the facility, only a vision of what it might look like. All of the renderings to date are conceptual and subject to change. The budget for the ESIF has been calculated at approximately $98 million, which includes the shell, structure, infrastructure improvements to the site, capital equipment, and high computing capabilities. The build-out schedule is as follows:

- Engage a design build firm in early 2009

- Finalize the design in 2009

- Begin construction in early 2010

- Occupy building in late 2011.

Functionality
The ESIF will be built as a state-of-the-art computational and experimental laboratory facility. Inclusion of a high performance computer is critical to the functionality of the ESIF. With the convergence of multiple, highly complex systems, the ability to identify where the real issues are and what the potential solutions are through a simulated environment where many simulations can be performed quickly, will be a key element in approaching integration challenges.

This high performance computer (with a 200 teraflop processing capacity) coupled with NREL's extensive information databases, particularly in the areas of resource measurements, resource forecasting, and temporal and spatial resolution, will provide increasingly complex simulations of the system from generating technologies to how they interact with the transmission systems, and furthermore, how transmissions and distributions interact. These solutions can then move to ESIF laboratories where prototypes can be developed to address the issues that were identified in the simulation—and at all times there remains that continual interplay between development of the prototype and the data from the simulated environment. Then, as the prototypes are refined and begin addressing the issues that were identified, they can then move to the outdoor and rooftop test bed environments to test their performance in a real environment.

A System of Systems
Historically, there has been an individualized approach to the physical systems of integration. Examples of individual components of energy systems can be categorized as:

Electricity System

- Generation Technologies

- Transmission Systems and Technologies

- Distribution Systems and Technology

- End use Technologies and the Built Environment.

Hydrogen Systems

- Energy source

- Electrolyzers

- Compressors

- Hydrogen Delivery Infrastructure

- Hydrogen Storage

- Generators

- Fuel Cells

One of the major challenges in building the ESIF is determining how these systems will interact up and down the infrastructure as high penetration of new technologies are introduced.

The not-too-distant future may bring a scenario with very high penetration, zero energy buildings, for example. One of the implications is that there will be a high percentage of photovoltaics (PV). To the system, low penetration of photovoltaics looks like a demand reduction technology. The power is confined to a building or neighborhood and has a similar effect of insulating homes, and utility companies do not have to provide as much power to these structures. In a high penetration scenario, however, one building, or even the entire neighborhood, cannot absorb all the power produced (especially if people are installing 6 kW systems in their homes) and will cause power flowing from the feeder to the substation. This is a very different operating environment for utility companies, and ESIF stakeholders should consider what kind of integration, interconnection, communication, and controls technologies need to be in place and what kind of operating techniques will be needed to accommodate that very new operating environment.

As an extension of this scenario, a very high penetration of "active distribution" technologies further in the future will cause the impact to revert all the way back to the central-station generation level. A high penetration of PV could potentially integrate with high numbers of plug-in hybrid electric vehicles and stationary fuel cells in the home, which require demand control technologies, smart grid technologies, and stationary storage. If power passes back through the substations, that puts a fairly significant amount of power out on the distribution system from distributed technologies. The substations are no longer demand reductions; they are actually generating electrons and kilowatt hours, which will impact how much power the generation and transmission operator needs to dispatch from the centralized system.

Critical Mission

Such a critical part of this integration mission stems from the development of these technologies from the innovation stage to the commercially deployable stage. If these issues do not address integration barriers and the ensuing challenges with operating this kind of system, all of the groundwork completed thus far to bring these technologies to commercialization will be hampered. The technology will be stymied by the inability to integrate solutions to these challenges into the infrastructure. So the critical mission of the EISF is to begin working with key stakeholders and start applying these capabilities to the interfaces of the system in order to allow higher penetration at faster rates.

The ESIF is not intended to be a facility in isolation. It can be much more effective with external stakeholders and other laboratories, universities, industries, and utilities, all working together.

3.2   ESIF Design Requirement Identification

Presented by Ben Kroposki, Group Manger, Distributed Energy Systems Integration, the ESIF Design Requirement Identification presentation explains the internal process NREL has engaged in so far to develop a baseline of functional capabilities and requirements of the facility.

Dr. Kroposki began this plenary session by explaining that the mission needs statement for the ESIF lists 13 specific competencies that describe the functionality and capability of the building.

The 13 competencies are:

1. Renewable resource characterization
2. Renewable systems operations and analysis support
3. Integrated testing and field validation of components
4. Simulation and development of system controls
5. Analyzing storage systems
6. Advanced energy computing capability
7. Renewable electricity production and hydrogen synergies
8. Buildings system integration
9. Market and integration analysis
10. Economic validation
11. Market competitiveness of zero energy buildings
12. Codes and standards
13. Combined heat and power

Approximately six months have been spent internally at NREL examining the 13 competencies and identifying the specific activities and tasks associated with them. As an example, Competency #2, Renewable Systems Operations and Analysis Support, was broken into several activities. One, for example, was to analyze distributed renewable energy systems. Each activity then was then broken down into specific tasks. So for this example, the tasks included to collecting renewable systems performance data and optimizing renewable system technoeconomic operations. By breaking each competency into specific activities and tasks, the requirements for space, equipment, and staff were determined at the lowest level. This methodology was conducted for all 13 competencies, which resulted in a total of 48 activities and 118 tasks. This internal process lead to the development of specific laboratories and functional space in the facility. The results from that exercise resulted in the following needs and cost assessments based on a bottoms-up approach.

Design Requirements

- Approximately 130,000 sq. ft.
  - 19 laboratories
  - 5 test facilities
  - ~200 person office capacity
  - Specialty areas
    - insight center including visualization rooms and collaboration areas
    - virtual control room for RE integration and infrastructure visualization
  - Common areas (building support, maintenance, conference rooms, security, ES&H, building management)
  - 15,000+ sq. ft. data center (with additional secure area)

Required Laboratories

Laboratory Name	Size (sq. ft.)
Manufacturing Lab	1,000
Photoelectrochemistry Hydrogen Lab	2,000
Fuels Quality Lab	1,000
High Pressure Lab	1,000
Components Lab	1,000
Hydrogen Production Lab	5,000
Fuel Cell Lab	2,000
Secure Data Center	1,500
High Bay Lab	10,000
Power Electronics Lab	1,800
Loads Lab	400
Energy Storage Lab	1,500
Electrical Visualization Lab	2,000

Laboratory Name	Size (sq. ft.)
High Voltage/High Current Lab	1,500
Instrument Development Lab	200
Roof Test Area	5,000
Outdoor Test Pads	
High Bay (VSHOT and ZEB)	7,000
Thermal Storage Materials Lab	1,000
Machine Shop	1,500
Electrical Shop	1,000
Conference Rooms	2,850
Office Space	17,500

Facility Cost Breakdown

- Total estimated cost: $98 million over three years of funding
  - $54.5 million in FY 2008
  - $4 million in FY 2009 - Infrastructure
  - $5 million in FY2009 - Other Costs
  - $34.5 million in FY 2010 - Equipment
    - $12 million High Performance Computer
    - $22 million in Equipment Capital

ESIF Build-out Schedule

Task	Status/Date
CD-0 (mission needs statement)	Approved May 2007
Received Funding ($55M)	October 2007
Define Internal User Requirements	July 2008
Define External user Requirements	October 2008
RFQ to Potential Bidders	September 2008
RFP to Potential Bidders	February 2009
CD-1 Package (base preliminary design)	June 2009
Select Design Build Contractor	August 2009
CD 2/3	January 2010
Construction Starts	February 2010
Construction Finishes	October 2011

3.3 Q&A following the ESIF Overview and Design Identification Presentations

What are you going to do to make the ESIF building itself a world-class, energy efficient building?

The ESIF is being designed to be LEED Gold certified. Creative ways to bring power to the building (i.e., hydrogen fuel cells, solar, etc.) are being explored. It will be a world-class building in terms of energy efficiency and renewable energy integration and use. One of the highest priorities is to make it an example that will show how to incorporate all of these efficiencies at a price that's not a premium to the rest of the industry. The high performance computer center is going to be the biggest challenge and external experts will be brought in for just that issue alone.

Seems like there's going to be a lot of challenges in working with your scientific staff, your high performance computing people, and the design build contractor. How are you going to handle the need for flexibility and continuous tweaking on the specifications during the design-build process?

A hybrid design build approach which separates the design build process into two phases will be used.

- The first phase is initiated after the design-builder acquisition stage is completed where the proposals are essentially conceptual designs and are based on performance requirements and specifications developed by NREL. Once through the competition stage, the first phase commences where intense collaboration with the selected design-build firm starts. This is a period of heavy collaboration with NREL researchers and other partners. This phase serves as an open book, real time estimating, value engineering, preliminary design where the best ideas of the design-builder are combined with NREL and partner's ideas. The ideas are estimated and designed into the facility. At the end of this phase, a firm-fixed price is offered by the design-builder for Phase II including a firm scope, schedule, and budget. The approach utilizes the Design Build Institute of America's Best Practices.

- The second phase then is to lock in the firm fixed price for the completion of design and construction of the facility consistent with the Phase I preliminary design.

Most importantly, during Phase I, the design is not just based on performance specifications, but the actual collaborations between the researchers and the design-build firm. This helps to identify efficiencies in the building process and maximize the energy efficiency and renewable energy integration. The result is consensus on the building and all of its capabilities in an integrated fashion.

As technology develops and changes, it's quite likely that we're going to have properties of that technology, for example storage or renewable generation, that don't match things like the national electric code. Do you have some way of being reasonably flexible because one of the things I see in energy storage is that we have to change the core requirements for safety and reliability for them to be able to accommodate new technology. What kind of flexibility do you foresee here?

NREL is a research facility and is constantly looking at new technologies that aren't going to meet specific codes and standards. While the building will be built around applicable building standards, research laboratories have that flexibility to test equipment that isn't meeting any particular standards because it is a research prototype. There is a very rigorous safety program at NREL to make sure that equipment and experiments are safe. This is especially true if the equipment is not listed or gone through a lot of testing before it gets to the laboratory.

To make sure the laboratories are safe operating places for this equipment to be evaluated, there are a lot of safety specifications that are built into the labs. It is expected that the ESIF will conduct testing of research prototype equipment with the adequate safety precautions.

This is also one of the benefits of the "hardware in the loop" that was discussed earlier. Hardware in the loop allows for the evaluation of research components in a simulated system environment. These simulations can be connected back to the larger data center for both data collection and monitoring as well as simulations using larger systems.

3.4   Renewable Resource Characterization
Presented by Tom Stoffel, Principal Group Manager, Resource Measurements & Forecasting

Renewable resources can vary considerably from one geographic location to another. Consequently, optimal technology selection, sizing, and siting of renewable energy systems require knowledge of the resource characteristics at any given location.

Current Activities
NREL's Resource Measurements & Forecasting Group provides high-quality renewable resource data for United States and international locations. The Quality Management & Systems Assurances Group is responsible for the development and operations of the NREL Metrology Laboratory. Some of the current activities being performed include:

- Developing and maintaining reference standards for electrical properties, pressure, radiometric, temperature, and time and frequency

- Calibrating measurement and test equipment

- Performing experiment design and measurement uncertainty analyses

- Providing nearly real-time surface meteorological and solar irradiance measurements

- Validating solar resource models used to estimate national and international resource climatologies (e.g., National Solar Radiation Database)

- Developing geographical information system (GIS) databases and visualization products for renewable energy R&D.

Future Activities
Future work will address the growing industry need for "bankable" (accurate and representative) resource data with higher temporal and spatial resolutions for global applications. This includes site-specific measurements of direct normal (beam), diffuse (sky), and total hemispheric solar irradiance, improved satellite remote sensing estimates of solar resources at ground level, and validation of solar resource forecasting methods.

Planned Lab Space to Support Renewable Resource Characterization Activities

Lab Name	Will provide...
Metrology Lab	Closer proximity to principal user-base of scientists and engineers responsible for measurement and test equipment; increased work space consistent with ISO accreditation goals; and a stable environment for reference standards.
GIS Lab	Improved access to data servers; a common area for applications development; map display, and data visualization hardware; and closer proximity to staff who need GIS services.

3.5 Distributed Systems Integration and Operation
Presented by Ben Kroposki, Group Manager, Distributed Energy Systems Integration

NREL's Distributed Energy Systems Integration Group conducts collaborative research and provides technical support that will enable the interconnection and integration of distributed energy resources (DER) with the electrical distribution system. DERs include a variety of distributed energy generation and storage technologies, including photovoltaics, wind, fuel cells, microturbines, engine/generators, batteries, flywheels, ultracapacitors, and vehicle-to-grid technologies.

Current Activities
Current R&D is focused on substation to load issues, with specific activities including, but not limited to:

- Renewable and distributed energy systems
    - Modeling, evaluation, and analysis of the impacts of high-penetration renewable and distributed energy
    - Development of distributed energy codes and standards
    - Regulatory and policy support for stakeholders
    - Modeling and development of advanced power electronics interfaces for DG and microgrid technology
    - Testing and evaluating interconnection equipment
    - Testing and evaluating SmartGrid technologies.
- Research on renewable electrolysis
    - Wind and photovoltaics to hydrogen via electrolysis

- o Testing and characterizing electrolyzers
- o Developing advanced power electronic interfaces.

Future Activities
Future activities will include:

- Modeling and testing integrated systems and optimization

- Moving beyond hardware in the loop testing to systems in the loop testing

- Analyzing large-scale deployments of renewable and distributed energy systems.

Planned Lab Space to Support Distributed Systems Integration and Operation Activities

Lab Name	Will provide...
Electrical Visualization Lab	The ability to show massively deployed renewable energy at the distribution level and monitor a simulated variety of energy generation, storage, use scenarios to understand impacts and optimizations.
High Bay	Accommodations for a 1 MW real-power grid simulator; wind and PV simulators; AC and DC test buses; many bays for DE systems with electrical, thermal, and fuel connections; and a large drive-in environmental chamber.
Outdoor Test Pads	Interconnection with a 13kV test circuit to allow distributed generation (up to 5MW) to be installed and tested.
Roof Test Area	A large PV array and test area.
Power Electronics Lab	Assistance in rapid prototyping and development of power electronic interfaces for renewable and distributed energy applications.
Loads Lab	A variety of building load capabilities to simulate residential and commercial scenarios.
Instrumental Development Lab	Advanced sensors for communications and control of distributed generation systems.
Energy Storage Lab	A variety of storage capabilities.
High Voltage/High Current Lab	Ability to conduct surge and fault testing on distributed generations.
Hydrogen Production Lab	A Class 1/Div 2 lab for electrolyzers interconnected to main electrical hub in high bay.

3.6   Transmission Systems Integration and Operation

Presented by Brian Parsons, Program Manager, Transmissions Systems Integration

For wind or other growing renewable energy markets to play a role in supplying the nation's energy needs, integrating that energy into the power grid of the United States is an important issue to address. NREL researchers are looking at improving the use of the existing transmission system particularly with regard to the effect on regulation, load following, scheduling, line voltage, reserves and reliability.

Current Activities

Current Transmission Systems Integration and Operation activities include:

- Wind generator dynamic stability modeling and validation
- Wind plant performance monitoring
- Grid markets and operational analysis and simulation
- Transmission analysis
- Stakeholder outreach, training, and education.

Future Activities

Future activities may include:

- Grid control room stimulator visualization
- Energy storage technology development and testing
- Potential grid operator training.

Planned Lab Space to Support Transmission Systems Integration & Operation Activities

Lab Name	Will provide...
Electrical Visualization Lab	The ability to show massively deployed renewable energy at the transmission level and monitor a simulated variety of energy scenarios to understand impacts and optimizations.
High Voltage/High Current Lab	Ability to conduct surge and fault testing on distributed generations.
GIS Lab	Improved access to data servers; a common area for applications development; map display, and data visualization hardware; and closer proximity to staff who need GIS services.
Visual Analysis Lab	
Metrology Lab	
High Performance Computing Capability Data Center	

3.7 Modeling, Simulation, and Data Management
Presented by Steven Hammond, Director, Computational Sciences Center

Modeling and simulation are intrinsic to conducting state-of-the-art research, complementing the two traditional scientific research methods of theory and experiment. A robust, high-performance computing capability is essential for NREL to achieve its mission. Modeling and simulation yield insight into physical phenomena occurring at time and length scales that elude direct observation or experimental techniques.

Current Activities
The Scientific Computing Center provides computing expertise to NREL and its subcontractors with a focus in three main areas:

- Numerical methods, algorithms, and simulation

- Data analysis and visualization

- Problem solving environments - integration of people, data, and instruments.

Current collaborations include projects designed to increase production of hydrogen and ethanol from renewable sources. Another project helps engineers analyze and optimize the efficiency of building heating, ventilation, and air-conditioning systems.

Planned Lab Space to Support Modeling, Simulation, & Data Mgmt. Activities

Lab Name	Will provide...
HPCC Data Center	High performance (100 teraflop) processing capabilities to assist in advancing scientific knowledge and engineering practices.
Insight Center Room	3D stereo visualization that will make complicated phenomena accessible and state-of-the-art video conferencing for collaboration with external industry, academia, and laboratory partners.

3.8 Buildings and Thermal Systems
Presented by Chuck Kutscher, Group Manager, Thermal Systems

NREL's Center for Buildings and Thermal Systems is organized into two major groups: the Buildings Research Group and the Thermal Systems Research Group. The buildings group conducts research in residential, commercial building technologies as well as thermally activated technologies. The thermal systems group conducts research in thermal power production, including concentrating solar power, solar heating and lighting, geothermal, and hydrogen.

Current Activities
Current Buildings and Thermal Systems activities include:
- Buildings
  - Zero energy buildings test and analysis
  - Solar Hot water system testing

14

- o PV/thermal hybrid testing
- o Advanced HVAC test lab.
- Thermal Systems
  - o Optical characterization of solar concentration systems
  - o Modeling and analysis of HTFs and thermal storage systems
  - o Grid integration/market analysis
  - o Solar resource measurement and forecasting.

Planned Lab Space to Support Buildings and Thermal Systems Activities

Lab Name	Will provide...
Buildings	
ZEB Lab	Workstations that utilize supercomputing capabilities for national impact simulations; an advanced system R&D lab; and a national ZEB cost/performance database.
Outdoor Test Pad	A place to evaluate full-scale building systems; .
Rooftop Test Area	A place to evaluate full-scale roof-mounted solar systems.
Instrument Development Lab	Staging and testing for building field monitoring instrumentation; a ZEB remote monitoring center; and a ZEB grid integration lab.
Thermal Systems	
Solar Concentrator Lab	Optical and structural load testing of large reflectors and mirror thermal cycling
Thermal Storage and HTF Materials Lab	Bench and floor space for analytical instruments and small-scale test systems.

3.9 Hydrogen Technologies
Presented by Robert Remick, Director, Hydrogen Technologies & Systems Center

NREL's Hydrogen Technologies & Systems Center is helping to facilitate the transition to a new energy future—a future built on diverse and abundant renewable resources and integrated renewable-hydrogen production systems. The Hydrogen Technologies Group is supporting the transition to a hydrogen energy future by contributing to several key research areas for engineering optimized energy systems.

Current Activities
Current R&D activities focus on:

- Hydrogen production – photoelectrochemistry
- Fuel cell components
- Manufacturing R&D
  - o Diagnostic techniques for in-line measurement of MEA components
  - o Impact of manufacturing defects on fuel cell performance

- Hydrogen properties and behavior
- Test hydrogen sensors
- Component R&D for integrated systems analysis
  - Storage cylinders
  - Ancillary equipment
- Technology Validation
  - Fuel cell passenger vehicles, transit buses, forklifts
  - Fueling infrastructure
- Analysis
  - Production pathways
  - Transition to hydrogen
  - Resource analysis
- Market transformation
  - Educational materials
  - Early adopter support.

Future Activities

Fuel cell R&D will be greatly expanded in the future to include electrode catalyst, catalyst support, and membrane development for Polymer Electrolyte Membrane (PEM) fuel cells. Water electrolysis work will be initiated and will include both PEM and high temperature ceramic electrolytes. Subsequently, the testing and electrical integration of prototype fuel cell and water electrolysis systems with the electric grid will be investigated and safety codes and standards established.

Planned Lab Space to Support Hydrogen Technology Activities

Lab Name	Will provide…
Outdoor Test Pad	A place to research and demonstrate hydrogen storage, compression, and dispensing equipment.
High Pressure Test Facility	The necessary equipment and space to evaluate integrated system components for the development of inherently safe building designs and containment vessels and system level components at high pressures.
Hydrogen Photoelectrochemistry Lab	A scale-up of photoelectrochemical hydrogen production and the ability to evaluate optimal integration of prototype and commercial hydrogen generation equipment with renewable electric generation equipment.
Fuel Cell Lab	The ability to integrate fuel cells into stationary and vehicles systems and research and run performance evaluations.

4 Breakout Session Details

Four separate breakout sessions convened after the general plenary session. Attendees were given the choice to participate in one of the four breakout groups based on their interest designated as follows:

- Electric Systems
- Building and Thermal Systems
- Hydrogen Systems
- Computational Sciences.

Each group was staffed with a facilitator and a note-taker and included representatives from a range of stakeholder groups. Participants were asked to focus on four major areas of design:

1. What are the top integration priorities that DOE and the ESIF should address to enable high penetration of energy efficiency and renewable energy technology?

2. How can the ESIF's design be best optimized to add value to your efforts in accelerating technology R&D, adoption, and integration?

3. Do we have the right functionality and set of capabilities identified to address the top integration priorities?

4. How can we best ensure sustained stakeholder input throughout the design/build and startup/fit-up process?

While there was significant overlap among the groups responses to these questions, each breakout group provided some unique suggestions and comments during the facilitated discussions.

4.1 Electric Systems
Facilitator: Ben Kroposki, Group Manager, Distributed Energy Systems Integration

Note-taker: Jennifer Elling, Technical Communications, NREL

In attendance:

Name	Title	Company	Field
John Boyles	Manager, Energy Infrastructure and DER	Sandia National Laboratories	Electricity
Greg Collett		DOE	
Dick DeBlasio	Program Manager	NREL	Electricity
Randy Dins		DOE	
Tien Duong		EERE	Electricity
Carolyn Elam		DOE	Hydrogen

Name	Title	Company	Field
Bill Foster	VP, Govt Operations	Fuel Cell Energy	Hydrogen
Ross Guttromson	Energy Science & Technology Division	Pacific Northwest National Laboratory	Electricity
Stephanie Hamilton	Distributed Energy Resources Transmission	Southern California Edison	Electricity
Donna Heimiller		NREL	Electricity
Ken Marken	Materials Science	Los Alamos National Laboratory	Hydrogen
Chris Marnay	Electricity Markets and Policy Group	Lawrence Berkeley National Laboratory	Electricity
Fernando Mancilla-David	Assistant Professor	University of Colorado	Electricity
Frank Novachek	Director of Corp. Business Dev.	Xcel Energy	Hydrogen
Joe Paladino		EERE	
Brian Parsons		NREL	Electricity
Redfoot	Application Engineer	EATON Corporation	Electricity
Drew Ronneberg		EERE	Hydrogen
Patrick Shipp		EERE	
Tom Stoffel	Principal Group Manager	NREL	Electricity
Siddharth Suryanarayanan	AP, Division of Engineering	Colorado School of Mines	Electricity

4.2 Building and Thermal Systems
Facilitator: Chuck Kutscher, Group Manager, Thermal Systems

Note-taker: Jennifer Josey, Technical Communications, NREL

In attendance:

Name	Title	Company	Field
Karri Bottom		NREL	
Kathye Chavez	Infrastructure Computing Systems	Sandia National Laboratories	Computing
Greg Glatzmaier	Senior Engineer	NREL	
Will Litner		DOE	
Nick Long	Engineer	NREL	
Dave Martinez		Sandia National Laboratories	Computing
Ram Narayanamurthy		Ice Energy	Buildings
Jim Rannels		EERE	Buildings
Dale Sartor		Lawrence Berkeley National Laboratory	Electricity
Otto VanGett		NREL	

4.3 Hydrogen Systems
Facilitator: Robert Remick and George Sverdrup, Hydrogen Technologies & Systems

Note-taker: Julie Tuttle, Technical Communications, NREL

In attendance:

Name	Title	Company	Field
Chad Blake		NREL	Hydrogen
Bill Foster	VP, Govt Operations	Fuel Cell Energy	Hydrogen
Ken Marken	Materials Science	Los Alamos National Laboratory	Hydrogen
Albert Migliori	Energy storage, and power systems	Los Alamos National Laboratory	Electricity
Frank Novachek	Director of Corp. Business Dev.	Xcel Energy	Hydrogen
Pinakin Patel	Director, Special Systems & Research	Fuel Cell Energy	Hydrogen
Patrick Shipp		EERE	
Jim Spaeth		DOE	
Robert Stokes	President	Versa Power Systems	Hydrogen

4.4 Computational Sciences

Facilitator: Steven Hammond, Director, Computational Sciences Center

Note-taker: Howard Brown, Technical Communications, NREL

In attendance:

Name	Title	Company	Field
Jim Albin	HPC System Administrator	NREL	Computing
Aaron Andersen	Enterprise Services Section Manager	National Center for Atmospheric Research	Computing
Karri Bottom		NREL	
Kathye Chavez	Infrastructure Computing Systems	Sandia National Laboratories	Computing
Randy Dins		DOE	
Matt Graham		DOE	
Ross Guttromsom	Energy Science & Technology Division	Pacific Northwest National Laboratory	Electricity
Wesley Jones		NREL	Computing
Dave Martinez		Sandia National Laboratories	Computing
Ram Narayanamurthy		Ice Energy	Buildings
Brent Nelson		NREL	Computing
Michael Patterson	Senior Power/Thermal Architect	Intel	Computing
Dale Sartor		Lawrence Berkeley National Laboratory	Electricity
Loren Toole	Superconductivity and Transmission	Los Alamos National Laboratory	Electricity
Otto VanGett		NREL	

5   Comparison Tables of Breakout Group Results

Note: Tables begin on following page.

5.1 What are the top integration priorities that DOE and the ESIF should address to enable high penetration of energy efficiency and renewable energy technology?

Electric Systems	Buildings & Thermal Systems	Computational Sciences	Hydrogen Systems

Determine impacts of higher penetration levels
• Quantify penetration limits for renewables and distributed energy. Better define levels that require system changes; identify steps and define plan to achieve higher levels
• Determine ramp rates for renewable technologies (i.e. for transient analysis, dynamic control, and integration with other generation sources)
• How to conduct contingency analysis with renewable systems
• How to determine reliability with integrated renewables. Determine how to analyze this issue
• Since utility systems differ, determine what can be considered as generic and what are specific differences between systems. Work with Utilities to get accurate data.
• How does revere power
	Buildings
	• Rooftop systems for solar thermal and PV/thermal hybrid systems
	• Well instrumented field test data from buildings around the country
	• Have parallel DC distribution system in building
	  – Use DC w/o inverter to get more power distribution (i.e., tie PV directly to enterprise computing)
	• Validate Energy Plus and BE opt via monitoring of real buildings
	  – Validation from building operation for broader applications
	• Smart Grid strategies to cut peak demand
	  – Adjust demand based on RE supply and experiments (Think models). i.e., pre-cool at night, as needed
	• Develop improved integrated control systems to optimize whole building
		• Provide New Capability: State-of-the-art, multi-program facility for computer simulation, scientific data management supporting experimental facilities, data mining, and high speed networks linking people, computers, data, and experiments.
		• Use the ESIF as a showcase for data center energy efficiency.
		• Move the industry to more efficient computing systems as well as data center users to more efficient designs.
		  – Higher allowable cooling temperatures and humidity.
		  – No mechanical cooling.
		  – "Cooling tower" based liquid cooled systems.
		• DC in the Data Center.
			• Evaluate options for tri-generation (hydrogen/electricity/heat) CHP&H_2
			• Integration of distributed generation technologies into electrical utility grids
			• Evaluate technologies for firming intermittent generation from renewables
			• Energy storage using reversible electrolyzer/fuel cell systems

5.1 What are the top integration priorities that DOE and the ESIF should address to enable high penetration of energy efficiency and renewable energy technology?

Electric Systems	Buildings & Thermal Systems	Computational Sciences	Hydrogen Systems

flow on distribution grid effect system protection and operations? What are these effects on the rest of the power system?
• What are the metrics that determine penetration levels?
Conduct Modeling, Testing and Evaluation of hardware
• Include the ability to conduct physical testing of current and advanced hardware as well as simulations of the components
• Be able to model and evaluate small systems and larger systems together (i.e. kW to MW)
• Determine the cost impacts of redeveloping distribution systems (infrastructure upgrades, etc) to utilities to handle distributed and renewable energy systems
Conduct Simulations and Analysis
• Economic values and business cases analysis
	performance
	• Real-time display ("dashboard") of energy use for commercial and residential buildings
	  - Effectiveness of displays; behavioral components
	  - Address usability needs for commercial and residential users
	• Needs slightly different for homeowners vs workers
	• Investigate ways that building operators can better accommodate dynamic utility rates ("real-time" pricing)
	• Need to understand, control, and redistribute energy used by building
	  - Mange energy use
	  - Expel or redistribute through the building, as applicable
	• Reduction of lighting loads
	  - Lighting represents 25-30% of loads according to DOE 2008 data book
	• Hydropower development simulations for impact on grid		

22

5.1 What are the top integration priorities that DOE and the ESIF should address to enable high penetration of energy efficiency and renewable energy technology?

Electric Systems	Buildings & Thermal Systems	Computational Sciences	Hydrogen Systems
from both the customer and utility perspective. ▪ Be able to evaluate a variety of scenario analysis quickly. This would allow customers and utilities to test implementation of strategies quickly before actual hardware implementation ▪ Be able to provide both component and overall system analysis (ex. Evaluate various rate structures, institutional and policy constraints, operational modes, determine how much and what type of base load generation is needed to match renewable; determine requirements to maintain system stability, etc.) *Implement solutions* ▪ Determine "grid friendly" solutions and standards for: – Maintaining the grid operations with variable generation and load	– Think offshore wind and run of river turbines *Thermal Systems* ▪ Storage needs ▪ Energy storage that is integrated w/grid needs (i.e., ice, phase change materials (PCM), compresses air, molten salt) ▪ Utility could have control over how ice storage is being used ▪ Match energy supply to demand ▪ Models needed so that simulation data looks the same ▪ Thermal testing on an outdoor pad ▪ Increasing the value and the timing of the energy that is being produced ▪ Better dispatchability		

23

5.1 What are the top integration priorities that DOE and the ESIF should address to enable high penetration of energy efficiency and renewable energy technology?

Electric Systems	Buildings & Thermal Systems	Computational Sciences	Hydrogen Systems
– Power quality including harmonics issue with inverters – how to handle/measure – Reactive power supply – Distributed storage – Interconnection points ▪ Determine the standards and codes changes that need to happen to allow high renewable penetration ▪ Develop a matrix of solutions to high penetration renewables based on mitigation efforts on specific issues			

24

5.2 How can the ESIF's design be best optimized to add value to your efforts in accelerating technology R&D, adoption, and integration?

Electric Systems	Buildings & Thermal Systems	Computational Sciences	Hydrogen Systems

Building Design Optimization
• Design and use ESIF as test bed (i.e. Consider DC connections to loads, configurable loads) to examine different options and keep as flexible as possible (i.e. lots of connections available, building hardware; rewiring building)
• Consider the lifecycle of building including flexibility for retrofits and expansions.
• Segment the building for various experiments and scenario analysis, such as response to demand mgmt; energy strategies, etc.
• Develop various levels of access to information and physical connections for partners.
• Design building to segregate loads by power quality/reliability requirements
• Aesthetics of building – make it a pleasant place to be in and to get around
• Define adequate office space for industry users
	Buildings
	• Building needs to be a "living lab" so that tech can be applied inside
	• Should be integral part of experiment
	• Improve equipment coordination
	• Rooftop test facility for both solar hot water, air, heating and cooling systems, and PV/thermal hybrid systems
	• Should integrate with grid emulator
	• Zero energy buildings lab
	• Field test layout and prototyping lab
	• Waste-Heat utilization lab
	• Advanced system R&D lab for ZEB activities
	• Improved space conditioning, ventilation, hot water distribution, standby losses
	• Must have physical access to roof to tie into rooftop systems
	• Calorimetry chambers for testing zero-energy buildings technologies
	• May also serve the purpose of environmental chamber
		• Provide outside access (Local governments, university campuses, industry) to models and data for more than just internal research efforts.
		  - EnergyPlus,
		  - Homer,
		  - PV Watts, etc.
		• Real-time dashboard to monitor instantaneous PUE (power usage effectiveness) and accumulative values.
		• PUE = Total Power / IT Equipment
		• Economizer hours, temperature profiles, allowable conditions.
			• Plug and play component testing facility for system components
			• Space for visiting collaborators - both offices and labs
			• Develop capabilities to investigate electrochemical separation and electrochemical compression of hydrogen
			• Visualization/simulation center for "What if" experiments
			• Microgrid elements onsite (e.g. wind turbine, PV, fuel cells)

5.2 How can the ESIF's design be best optimized to add value to your efforts in accelerating technology R&D, adoption, and integration?

Electric Systems	Buildings & Thermal Systems	Computational Sciences	Hydrogen Systems
Field Testing, Data Collection and Analysis Optimization • Make ESIF a public showcase both in terms of space and capability • Allow integration of onsite power with building; onsite storage; pre-cooling; etc. where possible. • Develop clear path from lab testing to field testing within building • Develop capability to partner with others to capture data from others field test sites • ESIF building performance data should be open and readily available • Examine the possibility of certification capability if it does not compete with industry. • Make sure building has the ability to provide segregation between competing technologies and protect proprietary information • Need to provide space separation for intellectual property development (both for hardware and	• Grid integration lab to investigate whole house control, smart meters, and reduction of peak loads • Instrumentation and submetering inside the building • Building Information Systems • Communicate what the building is supposed to do/intent • Tools that generate info that is useable • Keep everyone on track • Develop common plug-and-play protocol for equipment • Creation of mobile temporary lab spaces or "pods" • Could be used as mobile disaster recovery as well • Check during design phase for needless duplication in other labs • Sufficient flat outdoor pad space w/good sun exposure for test buildings • Pads should have high-speed data connection to ESIF and grid emulator and have related utility services • Closely coordinate building		

26

5.2 How can the ESIF's design be best optimized to add value to your efforts in accelerating technology R&D, adoption, and integration?

Electric Systems	Buildings & Thermal Systems	Computational Sciences	Hydrogen Systems
data) • Enough space to do "space heavy" testing of equipment but should not duplicate large space required testing (i.e. hydrogen tanks to destruction) and should coordinate with other labs and industry. • Provide advanced meter infrastructure analysis and communication systems between utilities and consumer and DE and loads • Provide protection in labs that deal with high current, short circuits, faults, etc (i.e. lightening strikes, etc) • Provide foundation of ground for stability of equipment that has vibration issues, etc. • Provide grounding capability for electric system • Provide sufficient water connections to equipment and consider water use	experiments, grid emulation work, and distributed generation (DG) work • Flexible design that allows for reconditioning of responses • Provide a lighting/daylighting lab that allows for testing of thermal impacts *Thermal Systems* • Nothing specific is needed for Buildings and Thermal Systems		

5.3 Do we have the right functionality and set of capabilities identified to address the top integration priorities?

Electric Systems	Buildings & Thermal Systems	Computational Sciences	Hydrogen Systems
ESIF should • Provide modeling capability and flexibility for various energy scenarios • Real time simulation and modeling (i.e. "hardware in the loop") capability • Have the ability to model and test advanced functionality of DER in order to help grid functionality instead of being detrimental • Test and evaluation capabilities for various system components and complete systems • Include a full range of simulators to consider all generation (PV, wind, turbines, fuel cells, and engines), storage, and loads (AC, household appliances, motors, drives, stray voltage, smart loads, startup current, frequency controlled loads, etc) • Have the ability to test and evaluate on site generation to provide ancillary services • Provide remote/external access to monitor and get	*Buildings* • "Data hub" for external/stakeholder use - Needs to be clear and user friendly - Security issues need to be addressed • Data classification will play a large role in accessibility • See questions 1 and 2 *Thermal Systems* • Nothing specific is needed for Buildings and Thermal Systems	• We have the opportunity to set aside a fraction of the data center for test and evaluation of new computing technologies with industry partners. – No clear mandate, no budget – Falls in the space between EE Programs (Buildings, Industrial Technology, Hydrogen, FEMP) • Needs further discussion	• In general, yes • Need capability for investigating hydrogen at pressures up to 12,000 psi • Flexibility to accommodate changing technologies and energy landscape

5.3 Do we have the right functionality and set of capabilities identified to address the top integration priorities?

Electric Systems	Buildings & Thermal Systems	Computational Sciences	Hydrogen Systems
feedback on testing. • Also define what is NOT going to be done at the ESIF as well (i.e. destructive testing, etc) • Don't compartmentalize technologies to help avoid stove pipes			

5.4 How can we best ensure sustained stakeholder input throughout the design/build and startup/fit-up process?

Electric Systems	Buildings & Thermal Systems	Computational Sciences	Hydrogen Systems

- Develop a website to show design/build progress (with FAQs). This would link to other facilities and collaborators
- Coordinate external design review group(s) to review particular parts of the building and similar group to integrate with whole design
- Solicit this large external stakeholder group to determine how involved they want to be
- Send out PowerPoint slides on major next steps/progress; hold follow up conference calls
- Show a Webcam of building progress
- Continue external coordination and know what other worldwide labs/entities are doing related to the ESIF mission (i.e. Japan – NEDO, FREEDM)
- Present information to the Gridwise Alliance/ Architecture council
	Buildings
	- Invite stakeholders to an initial design charrette
	- Programmatic requirements for labs and functionality
	- Energy design of the building itself
	- Have design meetings with appropriate stakeholders
	- After RFP goes out
	- After contractor selection but prior to any work being done
	Thermal Systems
	- The design of the ESIF is proceeding in parallel at this point
	- Keep DOE and industry participants involved
	- Involve wind experts in load testing
		- For the data center, we have engaged a broad constituency.
		  – NCAR
		  – LBNL
		  – Sandia
		  – Intel/Green Grid/ASHRAE
		  – PNNL
		  – LANL
		  – EE ITP and FEMP
		- Plans for ongoing teleconferences to address topics raised during this workshop.
		  – Waste heat utilization opportunities
		  – Vendor feedback meeting
			- Monthly e-newsletter to stakeholders
			- Review of preliminary design concept by stakeholders
			- Another workshop during the intensive design phase
			- Timely interaction between technical team members and stakeholders

6 Discussion on Collaboration and Industry Partnerships

Presented by Michael Pacheco, Vice President, Deployment & Industrial Partnerships, the open forum discussion on collaboration and industry partnerships encouraged feedback on how to better facilitate industry partnerships in order to increase and maximize the impact of the new Electric Systems Integration Facility.

Mike Pacheco began by asking the group to consider the full spectrum of a partnership—from idea conception, research, development, maturations, and early commercialization to large-scale deployment—and provide feedback as to what the key elements for an effective partnership strategy should be.

The general theme was that NREL's current collaboration model with industry tends to build off of a very large core of DOE technology that the lab has developed over the past years. Technology that has been developed by taxpayers dollars and is publicly available. Collaborations are then formed with industry when that technology moves into commercial practice. It's in this step that often times a partner will work with one of the labs and compete for dollars in a cost-share partnership. And while DOE and NREL play an active role in guiding the project, it's the industrial partner that really 'steers the ship.'

Looking forward, it's possible that the ESIF, and facilities like this, will create more opportunities to explore and develop different types of partnerships, specifically partnerships that are sometimes referred to as a pre-competitive partnerships or pre-competitive collaborations. There may be more opportunities to greatly leverage DOE's investment in the ESIF and their investment in the core research at NREL.

The real goal of a partnership like this is that it benefits the entire industry so that while the cost-sharing partners may gain some benefit (non-exclusive access or some lead time on the technology), the results, at some point in time, would be open to the entire industry without much delay.

After an entire day of talking about the ESIF, what it should be, and what characteristics is should have, the open forum discussion on Collaboration and Industry Partnerships began.

There was significant interest in both developing new models and taking advantage of models that DOE's Hydrogen and Vehicle Technologies Programs, DoD's Defense Advanced Research Projects Agency, SEMATECH, and other organizations have already developed, such as the Solid State Energy Convergence Alliance and the USAutoPARTS model.

Following the workshop, Pacheco obtained additional details on the partnership models used for SECA, Advanced Gas Turbine Systems Research Program (AGTSRP), USAutoPARTS Consortium, SEMATECH, and the new Engineering Technologies

Institute in the U.K. All of the models, and variations thereof, will be considered as tools to maximize the impact and value of the ESIF to industry.

Participants agreed that it is important to understand the barriers that face the industry and somehow work with state and local governments that are inclined to take an active role in aiding and assisting in deployment.

Industry partners also discussed that if they were to get together in a collaborative form with DOE, they would be willing to share in the cost of the work and it would be that "vested" interested that would give them the right to share in the direction of the work. Some inquired whether or not a type of model could be developed where a company could participate in a "knowledge-based" manner where partners could offer information or advice or suggestions based on their expertise and as a result benefit from the research findings in "real time" rather than waiting until the research project was finished and released to the public. It was noted that it would not be appropriate for a company that didn't physically contribute to the work or make a financial investment to get advanced knowledge about research results, particularly if they were results that could have an effect on a competitive situation in the business environment.

Key partnership model elements included:

- High-level, sponsor-defined outcomes

- A structure that meets the various requirements for all parties

- Deployment roadmaps.

Key barriers to partnerships like this included:

- Coming up with the cash for R&D

- Complex and time-consuming contracts

- Ensuring that, proportionally, each partner gets out what they put in.

Recommendations included looking at how trade organizations like ASHRAE, SEPA, and AWEA sponsor pre-competitive R&D.

Peer review panels were discussed where once project results are made public, a group of interested industry folks and stakeholders sit down together with DOE and NREL to review the significance of those results and in what direction future research is going. It was noted that these peer review panels can impact more than just what's going on at NREL. Discussions have been initiated in Washington, DC on NREL becoming a subcommittee to the National Advisory Board where industry members and utilities can engage in advising on integration issues on a national level.

Finally, the question was asked, "How important is it to you that we get this partnership modeling right?" Very important, was the response, because of the political support at the end of the day's funding. It is important to figure out a way to eliminate redundant spending and better leverage investments for the ESIF.

7 Closing Remarks

Presented by Robert Hawsey, Associated Lab Director, Electricity & End Use Systems, the closing remarks summarized key feedback topics that emerged throughout the day. Mr. Hawsey also thanks all of the participants for attending the workshop and assured them that their input is important in finalizing the design of the ESIF.

There is a coming convergence of the building system, transportation system, the built environment, and energy delivery systems, and evidenced by the issues in discussion throughout the day, several key factors need to be addressed in building a facility that encompasses the components of this union.

It was discussed that the ESIF building should be a living laboratory where the performance of the facility's components and systems will be the focus of the research conducted by its occupants. Next steps are to consider to what extent the ESIF will be a living laboratory and what types of features, such as onsite storage, advanced meter infrastructure, and submetering, need to be added to the design of the building to support this initiative.

From the "human" angle, there was fair amount of discussion about the interaction of people from utilities, industry, labs, and universities that will utilize the building and the energy efficient strategies of the building. Recommendations included benchmarking ideas from some of the stakeholder partners who have already incorporated a "human factors" design standard into their offices. For example, Southern California Edison's (SCE) Office of the Future, designed to be a sustainable building that saves energy while improving livability its employees.

Participants agreed that the ESIF outputs cannot simply be databases posted on the Internet. The ESIF needs to provide actionable and interactive information that informs and enables technology and integration decisions.

The ESIF design needs to ensure the appropriate balance between renewable and efficiency technology and utilize current partnerships (e.g., with Xcel, SCE) by taking advantage of their interest in distributed generation, intelligent demand-side controls, and demand response technologies.

The ESIF has a unique capability of enhancing its integration mission with the application of a System of Systems Model incorporating generation, transmission, and distribution technologies with end use technologies and the built environment.

The ESIF has the opportunity to reinvent how data centers are designed, built, and operated. The design of the high-performance computer and data center should establish benchmarks based on other labs (TEAM Initiative) for data center efficiency and rely on the U.S. Department of Energy's (DOE) Industrial Technologies Program (ITP) for decision tools and expertise. DC distribution to the computers should be explored and mechanical cooling should be eliminated. Novel techniques implemented that improve the energy performance of the data center should be broadly disseminated.

A key area of discussion surrounded partnering strategies or models that would be most effective in developing working partnerships at the ESIF. There was significant interest in both developing new models and taking advantage of models that DOE's Vehicle Technologies Program, DoD's Defense Advanced Research Projects Agency, and other organizations have already developed, such as the Solid State Energy Convergence Alliance and the USAutoPARTS model. Key model elements must include high-level, sponsor-defined outcomes and a structure that meets the various requirements for all parties. Recommendations also included looking at how trade organizations like ASHRAE, SEPA, and AWEA sponsor pre-competitive R&D.

Appendix A: Workshop Agenda

The Energy Systems Integration Facility
Stakeholders Workshop

October 9, 2008
Denver West Marriott – Golden Ballroom, Salon E
Golden, Colorado

7:30 – 8:00	Continental Breakfast
8:00 – 8:10	Welcome Remarks – Bob McGrath
8:10 – 8:35	ESIF Vision and Workshop Overview – Dave Mooney
8:35 – 9:00	ESIF Design Requirements Identification – Ben Kroposki
9:00 – 10:00	Topic Area Details

9:00 – 9:15	Renewable Resource Characterization – Tom Stoffel
9:15 – 9:30	Distributed Systems Integration and Operation – Ben Kroposki
9:30 – 9:45	Transmission Systems Integration and Operation – Brian Parsons
9:45 – 10:00	Modeling, simulation, and data management – Steve Hammond

10:00 – 10:20	Break
10:00 – 10:50	Topic Area Details, *continued*

10:20 – 10:35	Buildings and Thermal Systems – Chuck Kutscher
10:35 – 10:50	Hydrogen Technologies – Bob Remick

10:50 – 11:45 Breakout Discussions
- Electric Systems – Ben Kroposki and Brian Parsons
- Building and Thermal Systems – Chuck Kutscher
- Computational Sciences – Steve Hammond
- Hydrogen Systems – Bob Remick and George Sverdrup

11:45 – 1:15 Working Lunch
1:15 – 2:45 Breakout Discussions *Continued*
- Electric Systems – Ben Kroposki and Brian Parsons
- Building and Thermal Systems – Chuck Kutscher
- Computational Sciences – Steve Hammond
- Hydrogen Systems – Bob Remick and George Sverdrup

2:45 – 3:15	Break
3:15 – 4:00	Discussion on Collaboration and Industry Partnerships – Mike Pacheco
4:00 – 4:40	Reports from Breakout Discussions – Breakout Session Leader or Participant
4:40 – 5:00	Closing Remarks – Bob Hawsey

Appendix B: Workshop Attendance List

First Name	Last Name	Title	Company	Category	Field
Aaron	Andersen	Enterprise Services Section Manager	National Center for Atmospheric Research	Federal Gov	Computing
Chad	Blake		NREL	National Lab	Hydrogen
Karri	Bottom		NREL		
John	Boyles	Manager, Energy Infrastructure and DER	Sandia National Laboratories	National Lab	Electricity
Howard	Brown		NREL	National Lab	Communications
Gary	Burch		DOE	Federal Gov	Buildings
Kathye	Chavez	Infrastructure Computing Systems	Sandia National Laboratories	National Lab	Computing
Greg	Collett		DOE	Federal Govt	
Dick	DeBlasio	Program Manager	NREL	National Lab	Electricity
Drew	Detamore	Office Director	NREL	National Lab	Construction
Randy	Dins		DOE	Federal Gov	
Tien	Duong		EERE	Federal Gov	Electricity
Carolyn	Elam		DOE	Federal Gov	Hydrogen
Jennifer	Elling		NREL	National Lab	Communications
Steve	Ettinger		NREL	National Lab	
Bill	Foster	VP, Gov. Operations	Fuel Cell Energy	Industry	Hydrogen
Dale	Gardner		NREL	National Lab	Hydrogen
Bobi	Garrett		NREL	National Lab	Electricity
Jesse	Geiger		NREL	National Lab	

First Name	Last Name	Title	Company	Category	Field
Matt	Graham		DOE	Federal Gov	
Ross	Guttromson	Energy Science & Technology Division	Pacific Northwest National Laboratory	National Lab	
Stephanie	Hamilton	Distributed Energy Resources Transmission	Southern California Edison	Utility	Electricity
Steve	Hammond	Center Director	NREL	National Lab	Computing
Charles	Hanley	PV/Solar	Sandia National Laboratories	National Lab	Electricity
Bob	Hawsey		NREL	National Lab	Electricity
Donna	Heimiller		NREL	National Lab	Electricity
Wesley	Jones		NREL	National Lab	Computing
Jennifer	Josey		NREL	National Lab	Communications
Connie	Komomua		NREL	National Lab	Communications
Ben	Kroposki		NREL	National Lab	Electricity
Will	Lintner		DOE	Federal Gov	
Ken	Marken	Materials Science	Los Alamos National Laboratory	National Lab	Hydrogen
Chris	Marnay	Electricity Markets and Policy Group	Lawrence Berkeley National Laboratory	National Lab	Electricity
Dave	Martinez		Sandia National Laboratories	National Lab	Computing
Bob	McGrath		NREL	National Lab	
Albert	Migliori	Energy storage, and power systems	Los Alamos National Laboratory	National Lab	Electricity
David	Mooney	Center Director	NREL	National Lab	Electricity
Ram	Narayanamurthy		Ice Energy	Industry	Buildings

First Name	Last Name	Title	Company	Category	Field
Brent	Nelson		NREL	National Lab	Computing
Frank	Novachek	Director of Corp. Business Dev.	Xcel Energy	Utility	Hydrogen
Joe	Paladino		EERE	Federal Govt	
Brian	Parsons		NREL	National Lab	Electricity
Pinakin	Patel	Director, Special Systems & Research	Fuel Cell Energy	Industry	Hydrogen
Micheal	Patterson	Senior Power/Thermal Architect	Intel	Industry	Computing
Bill	Prymak		DOE	Federal Govt	
Jim	Rannels		EERE	Federal Govt	Buildings
Rob	Redfoot	Application Engineer	EATON Corporation	Industry	Electricity
Bob	Remick	Center Director	NREL	National Lab	Hydrogen
Drew	Ronneberg		EERE	Federal Govt	Hydrogen
Dale	Sartor		Lawrence Berkeley National Laboratory	National Lab	Electricity
Patrick	Shipp		EERE	Federal Govt	
Neil	Shyder		NREL	National Lab	
Marty	Smith	Manager, Environmental Policy	Xcel Energy	Utility	Electricity
Jim	Spaeth		DOE	Federal Govt	
Tom	Stoffel	Principal Group Manager	NREL	National Lab	Electricity
Robert	Stokes	President	Versa Power Systems	Industry	Hydrogen
Siddharth	Suryanarayanan	AP, Division of Engineering	Colorado School of Mines	University	Electricity

First Name	Last Name	Title	Company	Category	Field
George	Sverdrup	Laboratory Program Manager	NREL	National Lab	Hydrogen
Daniel	Sze		EERE	Federal Govt	Hydrogen
Pete	Theisen	Principal Engineer	EATON Corporation	Industry	Electricity
Loren	Toole	Superconductivity and Transmission	Los Alamos National Laboratory	National Lab	Electricity
Paul	Torcellini	Section Supervisor	NREL	National Lab	Buildings
Julie	Tuttle		NREL	National Lab	Communications
Otto	VanGeet		NREL	National Lab	
Ed	Vineyard		Oak Ridge National Laboratory	National Lab	

REPORT DOCUMENTATION PAGE

1. REPORT DATE (DD-MM-YYYY)	2. REPORT TYPE	3. DATES COVERED (From - To)
January 2009	Workshop Proceedings	

4. TITLE AND SUBTITLE	5a. CONTRACT NUMBER
Energy Systems Integration Facility (ESIF) External Stakeholders Workshop: Workshop Proceedings	DE-AC36-08-GO28308
	5b. GRANT NUMBER
	5c. PROGRAM ELEMENT NUMBER

6. AUTHOR(S)	5d. PROJECT NUMBER
C. Komomua, B. Kroposki, D. Mooney, T. Stoffel, B. Parsons, S. Hammond, C. Kutscher, R. Remick, G. Sverdrup, R. Hawsey, and M. Pacheco	NREL/ TP-581-44249
	5e. TASK NUMBER
	IGIN.7400
	5f. WORK UNIT NUMBER

7. PERFORMING ORGANIZATION NAME(S) AND ADDRESS(ES)	8. PERFORMING ORGANIZATION REPORT NUMBER
National Renewable Energy Laboratory 1617 Cole Blvd. Golden, CO 80401-3393	NREL/ TP-581-44249

9. SPONSORING/MONITORING AGENCY NAME(S) AND ADDRESS(ES)	10. SPONSOR/MONITOR'S ACRONYM(S)
	NREL
	11. SPONSORING/MONITORING AGENCY REPORT NUMBER

12. DISTRIBUTION AVAILABILITY STATEMENT
National Technical Information Service
U.S. Department of Commerce
5285 Port Royal Road
Springfield, VA 22161

13. SUPPLEMENTARY NOTES

14. ABSTRACT (Maximum 200 Words)
On October 9, 2008, NREL hosted a workshop to provide an opportunity for external stakeholders to offer insights and recommendations on the design and functionality of DOE's planned Energy Systems Infrastructure Facility (ESIF). The goal was to ensure that the planning for the ESIF effectively addresses the most critical barriers to large-scale energy efficiency (EE) and renewable energy (RE) deployment. This technical report documents the ESIF workshop proceedings.

15. SUBJECT TERMS
ESIF; Energy Systems Infrastructure Facility; NREL; external stakeholders workshop proceedings

16. SECURITY CLASSIFICATION OF:			17. LIMITATION OF ABSTRACT	18. NUMBER OF PAGES	19a. NAME OF RESPONSIBLE PERSON
a. REPORT	b. ABSTRACT	c. THIS PAGE	UL		
Unclassified	Unclassified	Unclassified			**19b. TELEPHONE NUMBER** (Include area code)

CPSIA information can be obtained at www.ICGtesting.com
Printed in the USA
BVOW07s1448040514

352422BV00007B/236/P